Sisters

So Much We Share

Copyright © 1995
Brownlow Publishing Company
6309 Airport Freeway
Fort Worth, Texas 76117

The ribbon and associated ornamentation
on this product are proprietary
and are trademarks of the Publisher
and are protected by Federal and State Law.

ISBN 1-57051-051-2

Cover/Interior:
Koechel Peterson & Associates

Printed in USA

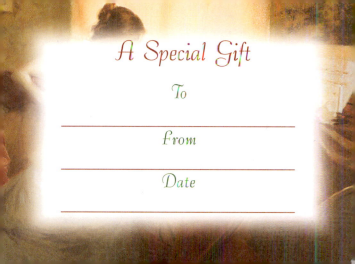

A Special Gift

To

_____

From

_____

Date

_____

Little Ribbons of Love

Afternoon Tea: Making Memories With Friends

Angels: Ever In Our Midst

Flowers for a Friend

Sisters: So Much We Share

Sisters

So Much We Share

Brownlow

Brownlow Publishing Company, Inc.

Sisters—So Much We Share

Growing up, sisters really do share so much. They share the same memories, the same household chores, the same holiday traditions, the same relatives, the same clothes, and often the same room.

And while time and age give to each sister some new experiences, even these get "shared" as one story after another comes tumbling out when they get together.

But ultimately, sisters share more than just time and space together; they share their hearts.

A sister is quick to defend you and slow to judge you.

What different lives we should lead if we would but take things by the minute!

GILBERT-ANN TAYLOR

*F*or one human being to love another;
that is perhaps the most difficult of
all your tasks, the ultimate, the last
test and proof, the work for which all
other work is but preparation.

RAINER MARIA RILKE

Home is the one place in all this world where hearts are sure of each other. It is the place of confidence. It is the place where we tear off that mask of guarded and suspicious coldness which the world forces us to wear in self-defense, and where we pour out the unreserved communications of full and confiding hearts. It is the spot where expressions of tenderness gush out without any sensation of awkwardness and without any dread of ridicule.

FREDERICK W. ROBERTSON

Our Lord does not care so much
for the importance of our works
as for the love with which they
are done.

TERESA OF AVILA

I've been on a diet for two weeks and all *I*'ve lost is two weeks.

TOTIE FIELDS

Sincerity is an openness of heart; we find it in very few people.

FRANÇOIS, DUC DE LA ROCHEFOUCAULD

Often, in old age, [sisters] become each other's chosen and most happy companions. In addition to their shared memories of childhood and of their relationship to each other's children, they share memories of the same home, the same homemaking

style, and the same small prejudices
about housekeeping that carry the
echoes of their mother's voice.

MARGARET MEAD

To understand any living thing
you must creep within
and feel the beating of its heart.

W. MACNEILE DIXON

If I could, I would always work in silence and obscurity, and let my efforts be known by their results.

EMILY BRONTË

Kind Words

Kind words toward those you daily meet,
Kind words and actions right,
Will make this life of ours most sweet,
Turn darkness into light.

ISAAC WATTS

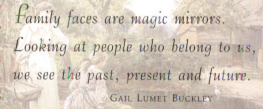

Family faces are magic mirrors.
Looking at people who belong to us,
we see the past, present and future.

GAIL LUMET BUCKLEY

*A heart at peace
gives life to the body*

PROVERBS 14:30

Without hearts there is no home.

LORD BYRON

My Sister

My sister! my sweet sister!
if a name
Dearer and purer were,
it should be thine.

Lord Byron

Living in the lap of luxury
is pretty good, except that you
never know when luxury
is going to stand up.

Each woman *has* a *choice* in life:
She *may* approach it as a creator
or critic, a lover or a hater,
a giver or a taker.

UNKNOWN

*L*ove is the one ingredient of which our world never tires and of which there is never an abundance. It is needed in the marketplace and in the mansions. It is needed in the ghettos and in the governments. It is needed in homes, in hospitals, and in individual hearts. The world will never outgrow its need for love.

C. NEIL STRAIT

One of life's major mistakes is being the last member of the family to get the flu—after all the sympathy has run out.

A woman should always stand by a woman.

EURIPIDES

I can never close my lips
where I have opened my heart.

CHARLES DICKENS

A family is a unit composed
not only of children, but of men,
women, an occasional animal,
and the common cold.

OGDEN NASH

The Three Sisters

Gone are those three, those sisters rare
With wonder-lips and eyes ashine.
One was wise, and one was fair,
And one was mine.

ARTHUR DAVISON FICKE

Cheerfulness is the atmosphere
in which all things thrive.

JOHANN PAUL RICHTER

The way to love anything
is to realize that it might be lost.

G. K. CHESTERTON

Half of the world is on the wrong scent in the pursuit of happiness. They think it consists in having and getting, and in being served by others. It consists in giving and in serving others.

HENRY DRUMMOND

God washes the eyes by tears until
they can behold the invisible land
where tears shall come no more.

HENRY WARD BEECHER

We find rest in those we love,
and we provide a resting place in
ourselves for those who love us.

BERNARD OF CLAIRVAUX

Family jokes, though rightly cursed by strangers, are the bond that keeps most families alive.

STELLA BENSON

Nostalgia is remembering the pleasures of our old kitchen when we were kids, without remembering how long it took to wash the dishes.

My sister and my sister's child,
Myself and children three,
Will fill the chaise; so you must ride
On horseback after we.

WILLIAM COWPER

I've got a woman's ability to stick to a job and get on with it when everyone else walks off and leaves it.

MARGARET THATCHER

*Great thoughts come
from the heart.*

MARQUIS DE VAUVENARGUES

You should remember that though another may have more money, beauty, and brains than you, yet when it comes to the rarer spiritual values such as charity, self-sacrifice, honor, nobility of heart, you have an equal

chance with everyone to be the most
beloved and honored of all people.

ARCHIBALD RUTLEDGE

The finger of God points to home, and says to us all, "There is the place to find your earthly joy!"

Better do a good deed
near at home than go far away
to burn incense.

CHINESE PROVERB

*Let parents bequeath
to their children not riches,
but the spirit of reverence.*

PLATO

According to popular myth, sisters
exist on the same side of the closed
door, sharing teddy bears and secrets
in the privacy of a common bedroom.

MARIANNE PAUL

A sister is both your mirror—

and your opposite.

ELIZABETH FISHEL

*M*ore important than length of life
is how we spend each day.

MARIA A. FURTADO

Two Hearts

Two souls with but a single thought,
Two hearts that beat as one.

VON MÜNCH BELLINGHAUSEN

Bringing up a family should be an adventure, not an anxious discipline in which everybody is constantly graded for performance.

MILTON R. SAPIRSTEIN

One is not born a woman,

one becomes one.

SIMONE DE BEAUVOIR

The pleasantest things in the world
are pleasant thoughts.

BOVEE

It is a terrible—*and I* mean terrible—nuisance to be kin to the president of the *United* *States.*

HARRY S. TRUMAN
(to his sister two weeks after becoming President)

It probably would be all right if we'd love our neighbors as we love ourselves, but could they stand that much affection?

*I*t is surely better to pardon

too much than to condemn too much.

GEORGE ELIOT

Cheerful Hearts

I am glad to think
I am not bound to make the wrong
  go right;
But only to discover, and to do,
With cheerful heart, the work that
God appoints.

JEAN INGELOW

A true sister is a friend who listens with her heart.

ANONYMOUS

*T*ears are the safety valve of the heart when too much pressure is laid on.

ALBERT SMITH

She wore age so gracefully, so carelessly, that there was a sacred beauty about her faded cheek more lovely and lovable than all the bloom of her youth. Happy woman! who was not afraid of growing old.

DINAH MARIA MULOCK CRAIK

It's a great comfort
to have an artistic sister.

LOUISA MAY ALCOTT

I never ask the wounded person how he feels; I myself become the wounded person.

WALT WHITMAN

There is an essential meanness in the wish to "get the better of" any one. The only competition worthy of a wise woman is with herself.

MRS. JAMESON

Home

Home is where affections bind
Gentle hearts in union,
Where voices all are kind,
Together holding sweet communion.

The advantage of a large family
is that at least one of the children
may not turn out like the others.

If life were predictable

it would cease to be life

and be without flavor.

ELEANOR ROOSEVELT

She had come to be a friend and companion such as few possessed— intelligent, well-informed, useful, gentle, knowing all the ways of the family, *interested in all its concerns, and peculiarly interested in Emma, in every pleasure, every scheme of hers; one to whom Emma could speak every thought as it arose, and who had such an affection for her as could never find fault.*

JANE AUSTEN

Be completely humble and gentle;
be patient, bearing with one another
in love.

EPHESIANS 4:2

Have a heart that never hardens,
and a temper that never tires,
and a touch that never hurts.

CHARLES DICKENS

There can be no situation in life in which the conversation of my dear sister will not administer some comfort to me.

LADY MARY WORTLEY MONTAGU

A happy family
is but an earlier heaven.

SIR JOHN BOWRING

The cheapest of all things is kindness,
its exercise requiring the least possible
trouble and self-sacrifice.

SAMUEL SMILES

Call it a clan, call it a network, call it a tribe, call it a family. Whatever you call it, whoever you are, you need one.

JANE HOWARD

No Friend Like a Sister

For there is no friend like a sister,
In calm or stormy weather,
To cheer one on the tedious way,
To fetch one if one goes astray,
To lift one if one totters down,
To strengthen whilst one stands.

CHRISTINA ROSSETTI

Men live by forgetting—

women live on memories.

T. S. ELIOT

A sister is a gift of God, sent from above to make life worthwhile here below.

It is not required of every man
and woman to be or to do something
great; most of us must content
ourselves with taking small parts
in the chorus, as far as possible
without discord.

HENRY VAN DYKE

What lies behind us, and what lies before us are tiny matters, compared to what lies within us.

RALPH WALDO EMERSON

Sisters is probably the most competitive relationship within the family, but once the sisters are grown, it becomes the strongest relationship.

MARGARET MEAD

A ministering angel shall

my sister be.

WILLIAM SHAKESPEARE

*W*arm your body by healthful exercise, not by cowering over a stove.

HENRY DAVID THOREAU

What families have in common
the world around is that they
are the place where people learn who
they are and how to be that way.

Jean Illsley Clarke

The woman who creates and sustains a home, and under whose hands children grow up to be strong and pure men and women is a creator second only to God.

HELEN HUNT JACKSON

Charity begins at home but should not end there.

I avoid looking forward or backward, and try to keep looking upward.

CHARLOTTE BRONTË

The family—that dear octopus from whose tentacles we never quite escape, nor, in our inmost hearts, ever quite wish to.

DODIE SMITH

Just in case I never told you,

I'm grateful to have you

for my sister, my friend.